ARE YO

300 MANCHESTER UNITED F.C. QUIZ QUESTIONS

BY

SEBASTIAN CARPENTER

Eaglestar Books

First published by Eaglestar Books, 2020

This Continental Edition first issued by Eaglestar Books in paperback and digital edition

© Sebastian Carpenter, 2020

Printed in Great Britain

Eaglestar Books

PO Box 7086

Harrow, London

HA2 5WN, United Kingdom

To all of the players and staff, past and present, who have worked for and dedicated themselves to the success of the club during its remarkable history.

TABLE OF CONTENTS

Preface

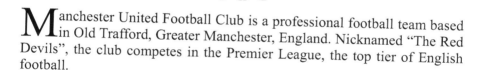

Manchester United Football Club is a professional football team based in Old Trafford, Greater Manchester, England. Nicknamed "The Red Devils", the club competes in the Premier League, the top tier of English football.

There are very few clubs in the history of football that can boast of as illustrious a history as Manchester United F.C. The club has performed consistently well over the years, and established itself as one of the biggest clubs in the English Premier League and indeed, the world.

It is this very stature that has contributed to the club's unbelievable popularity amongst fans all around the globe.

The glory years epitomise Man Utd's success, from Sir Matt Busby who was the first manager of an English team to win the European Cup and who is widely regarded as one of the greatest managers in history; to the appointment of Sir Alex Ferguson in 1986. During Fergie's 26 year reign at United, he won 38 trophies, including 13 Premier League titles, 5 F.A. Cups, and 2 UEFA Champions League titles.

The book also features questions on United facts, trivia, memorable moments from over the years; as well as numerous fan-favourite players such as: Dennis Law, George Best, Bryan Robson, Eric Cantona, Roy Keane, and Cristiano Ronaldo to name but just a few.

"The high point of my career was winning the Champions League. No one will ever erase that from my memory, in the same way that no one will ever erase the fact that I did it in a Manchester Unites shirt." ~ Cristiano Ronaldo.

Enjoy the book!

Chapter 1
Round One Quiz Questions

Round One Quiz Questions 1-15:

1. Sir Alex Ferguson was appointed manager of Manchester United in 1986 after his predecessor was sacked, who was this predecessor?

2. Who scored three hat-tricks in the 2010/11 season against Liverpool, Blackburn Rovers and Birmingham City?

3. Which United player retired in 2003 with an international career total of 129 caps and 1 goal?

4. Where was Ryan Giggs born?

5. Who did United sign from PSV Eindhoven back in April 2001?

6. During the 1968 European Cup Final, who scored United's first goal uncharacteristically with his head?

7. What is Mark Hughes' nickname?

8. Against whom did Andy Cole score his first league goal at Old Trafford?

9. Which ex-United player had the Spanish nickname "Chicharito"?

10. Who was the captain of United during the inaugural 1992/93 season?

11. In 2014, which former fans' favourite managed a Welsh team?

12. Which three United players were in England's 2016 squad?

13. Who were United's shirt sponsors from 1982-2000?

14. Shortly after leaving Manchester United, which team did Eric Cantona captain?

15. Which two United players featured in England's 1966 winning World Cup team?

FIND THE ANSWERS
ON THE
NEXT PAGE!

Round One Answers 1-15

1. Ron Atkinson.
2. Dimitar Berbatov.
3. Peter Schmeichel.
4. Cardiff.
5. Ruud Van Nistelrooy.
6. Bobby Charlton.
7. Sparky.
8. Manchester United.
9. Javier Hernandez; Little Pea.
10. Bryan Robson.
11. Ole Gunnar Solskjaer.
12. Chris Smalling, Marcus Rashford, and Wayne Rooney.
13. Sharp.
14. France's national beach football team.
15. Bobby Charlton and Nobby Styles.

Round One Quiz Questions 16-30:

16. Which club did United sign Antonio Valencia from?

17. Who scored 24 league goals in his first season after signing from Celtic in 1987?

18. Name the United player that won English Footballer of the Year and PFA Player of the Year in 2000?

19. What was the transfer fee when Juan Sebastián Verón joined from Lazio 2001?

20. Who transferred from Norwich City in December 1987 for £825,000?

21. Which player scored the first Premier League goal at Old Trafford in a 3-0 defeat to Everton?

22. Who became United's record signing in the summer of 2002?

23. What was George Best's nickname?

24. Which United player scored a hat-trick on his debut against Fenerbahce in 2004?

25. Where did United sign Frank Stapleton from for £900,000 in August 1981?

26. Who made 206 consecutive league appearances for the Red Devils between 1977 and 1981?

27. Which team suffered an 8-2 defeat at the hands of United in the 2011/12 campaign?

28. Name the four United players who have won European

Footballer of the Year?

29. Who had stints with Mallorca and Atlético Madrid before joining United in 1999?

30. Which player made their United debut in a goalless draw at home to Wolverhampton Wanderers on 1 February 2020?

FIND THE ANSWERS
ON THE
NEXT PAGE!

9

Round One Answers 16-30

16. Wigan Athletic.
17. Brian McClair.
18. Roy Keane.
19. £28.1 million.
20. Steve Bruce.
21. Peter Beardsley.
22. Rio Ferdinand.
23. El Beatle.
24. Wayne Rooney.
25. Arsenal.
26. Steve Coppell.
27. Arsenal.
28. Denis Law (1964), Bobby Charlton (1966), George Best (1968), Cristiano Ronaldo (2008).
29. Quinton Fortune.
30. Bruno Fernandes.

Round One Quiz Questions 31-50:

31. Name the former United player who finished their playing career at Fort Lauderdale Strikers in 2016?

32. On 21 September 1994, which United legend scored both goals in a 2-1 victory over Port Vale in the Football League Cup?

33. Bobby Robson signed which former United player for Newcastle United for a fee of £2.5 million where he was seen as a replacement for Gary Speed?

34. United's 40 year old, 56 match unbeaten home record finally came to an end in the 1996/97 tournament to which team?

35. In April 1992, United had to beat Liverpool at Anfield to stay in contention for the title. They lost out 2-0, who scored the goals for Liverpool?

36. Which ex-United player began their career with Cerezo Osaka in 2006?

37. From which English coastal club did Lee Sharp join?

38. Jaap Stam, Dwight Yorke and which other player was signed in the pre-season for the 1998/99 campaign?

39. Who joined from Chelsea for £825,000 in August 1979?

40. Manchester United became the first British club to win the FIFA Club World Cup with Wayne Rooney scoring the only goal, who did they beat?

41. Sir Alex Ferguson once said "He'll get me 15 goals this season, and what's more, they'll be important goals". Who was he talking about back in 2007?

42. Which player scored the winning goal for United in the second leg of the 1999 Champions League Semi-Final against Italian giants Juventus?

43. Who signed for Inter Milan in 1995 after leaving United?

44. Which Man Utd player scored against the same goalkeeper, Gordon Banks, for 3 different teams?

45. After the first game ended in a draw, who did United beat to reach the 1990 F.A. Cup Final?

46. Who scored to clinch the title for Arsenal at Old Trafford in the 2001/02 season?

47. The first player from outside of the United Kingdom and Republic of Ireland to captain United was whom?

48. Despite scoring 23 league goals in the 2001/02 season, which player pipped Ruud van Nistelrooy's efforts?

49. Where did United sign Ole Gunnar Solskjær from?

50. Which team knocked Manchester United out of the European Champions League in April, 2000 with a 3-2 victory?

FIND THE ANSWERS
ON THE
NEXT PAGE!

Round One Answers 31-50

31. Kléberson.
32. Paul Scholes.
33. Nicky Butt.
34. Fenerbahçe.
35. Ian Rush and Mark Walters.
36. Shinji Kagawa.
37. Torquay.
38. Jesper Blomqvist.
39. Ray Wilkins.
40. LDU Quito.
41. Carlos Tevez.
42. Andy Cole.
43. Paul Ince.
44. Denis Law.
45. Oldham Athletic.
46. Sylvain Wiltord.
47. Eric Cantona.
48. Thierry Henry.
49. Molde.
50. Real Madrid.

Round One Quiz Questions 51-65:

51. United won the 2016 F.A. Cup Final against Crystal Palace with an extra-time winner, who scored it?

52. Who was the oldest player to play for United at 40 in the post-war period?

53. What year did Cristiano Ronaldo sign for United?

54. Steve Bruce signed for United from which team?

55. Against which team did United win 9-0 to claim their record highest victory?

56. Who was Sir Alex Ferguson's first club signing?

57. After Sir Matt Busby stepped down as United manager in 1969, who was his replacement?

58. Which team did George Best score six goals against in 1970?

59. Who was brought in as a replacement for Mark Bosnich and Raimond van der Gouw, but was dubbed "The Blind Venetian" after several high-profile mistakes?

60. After scoring on his debut against Southampton, which player went on score 7 goals in his first 10 starting appearances for United?

61. After scoring an equaliser in extra-time against Crystal Palace in the 1994/95 F.A. Cup Semi-Final at Villa Park, which player then went on to score again when United won the replay?

62. After being unable to break into his preferred position at centre-back, which player was often used as a replacement right-back for Paul Parker in his first season at United?

63. Who did United sign for £36 million (potentially rising to £58 million) from AS Monaco on 1 September 2015?

64. Sir Alex Ferguson stepped down as Manchester United manager after 27 years in charge. Who was his last game in charge against that saw a memorable 5-5 result at the end of the 2012/13 season?

65. Mikaël Silvestre joined United for £1 million in July 1999, where did he sign from?

FIND THE ANSWERS
ON THE
NEXT PAGE!

51. Jesse Lingard.
52. Edwin van der Sar.
53. 2003.
54. Norwich City.
55. Ipswich Town.
56. Viv Anderson.
57. Ralph Milne.
58. Northampton Town.
59. Massimo Taibi.
60. Louis Saha.
61. Gary Pallister.
62. David May.
63. Anthony Martial.
64. West Bromwich Albion.
65. Inter Milan.

Round One Quiz Questions 66-80:

66. Which team did Peter Schmeichel sign for after leaving United in 1999?

67. During a match against Liverpool in February 2006, which former United player broke their leg?

68. Which former United player known as "Big Norm" retired from football at the age of 26?

69. Who set up the dramatic injury-time winner for United against Bayern Munich in the Champions League Final?

70. After retirement, which ex-United player took up an assistant managerial role with Trinidad & Tobago?

71. When did Newton Heath LYR Football Club change its name to Manchester United Football Club?

72. Who signed from Blackburn Rovers for £5 million in August 1997?

73. Where was former United assistant manager Carlos Queiroz born?

74. In August 1962 United signed Denis Law from which Club?

75. Who were United's sponsor after Sharp?

76. Schmeichel, Parker, Irwin, Bruce, Pallister, Cantona, Ince, Keane, Hughes, Giggs and which other player also started the 1994 F.A. Cup Final for Man Utd?

77. Who were United playing against when Mark Hughes scored his first senior hat-trick?

78. When Andy Cole joined Newcastle United, who was part of

an exchange deal that saw him go the opposite way?

79. By what nickname were United known during the late 1950's?

80. Which team beat United 6-3 in the 1996/97 season?

FIND THE ANSWERS
ON THE
NEXT PAGE!

Round One Answers 66-80

66. Sporting Lisbon.
67. Alan Smith.
68. Norman Whiteside.
69. Teddy Sheringham.
70. Dwight Yorke.
71. 1902.
72. Henning Berg.
73. Mozambique.
74. Torino.
75. Vodaphone.
76. Andrei Kanchelskis.
77. Aston Villa.
78. Keith Gillespie.
79. The Busby Babes.
80. Southampton.

Round One Quiz Questions 81-100:

81. Who was banned for 8 months in January 2004 for missing a routine drug test?

82. After making an inappropriate comment about Marcel Desailly live on air, which former United manager resigned from his job with ITV in April 2004?

83. What year did United win their first Premier League title?

84. In the days of 1-11 numbering of shirts, which Welsh player's versatility saw him wear every shirt number from 2-11?

85. A £1.2 million transfer fee in July 1994 saw which player move from Blackburn Rovers to United?

86. Who scored the "Goal of the Decade" on the opening day of the season against Wimbledon?

87. "Jaws" was the nickname of which Scottish footballer?

88. The winning goal in the 1990 F.A. Cup Final was scored by whom?

89. Who is the assistant manager of United as of the 2019/20 campaign?

90. The nickname "Choccy" was given to which player?

91. During the 1968 European Cup Semi-Final stage, which player scored a rare goal to help United progress to the final?

92. What shirt number did George Best sport most often for United?

93. When was the 'Munich Air Disaster'?

94. Where did United sign Andrei Kanchelskis from?

95. United were managed by whom when Bobby Charlton ended his career?

96. Sir Alex Ferguson took the helm at United in which year?

97. What was Bryan Robson's nickname?

98. On 27 June 2014, which player signed for United making him the most expensive teenager in the world?

99. Wayne Rooney and which other United player scored hat-tricks on their debuts?

100. Irish international Dennis Irwin joined from which club?

FIND THE ANSWERS
ON THE
NEXT PAGE!

81. Rio Ferdinand.
82. Ron Atkinson.
83. 1992/93.
84. Clayton Blackmore.
85. David May.
86. David Beckham.
87. Joe Jordan.
88. Lee Martin.
89. Mike Phelan.
90. Brian McClair.
91. Bill Foulkes.
92. Number 7.
93. 6th, February 1958.
94. Shakhtar Donetsk.
95. Tommy Docherty.
96. 1968.
97. Captain Marvel.
98. Luke Shaw.
99. Charles Sagar.
100. Oldham Athletic.

Chapter 2

Round Two Quiz Questions

Round Two Quiz Questions 101-115:

101. Which Norwegian won 4 league titles (1997, 1999, 2000, and 2001), and one F.A. Cup (1999) with United?

102. Gary Neville's autobiography is entitled what?

103. Roy Keane scored twice on his home debut for United in a 3-0 victory against who?

104. Who scored Bayern Munich's goal in the 1999 European Cup Final?

105. When was the club now known as Manchester United formed?

106. Which player played only two games for United before moving to Stoke City in 2008 for a £2 million fee?

107. Who became the head coach at F.C. Cincinnati?

108. Prior to joining United, which player was already friends with Portuguese speaking soon-to-be teammates Cristiano Ronaldo and Nani?

109. Who is the son of Rugby Union and Wales international rugby league footballer Danny Wilson?

110. Where did David Moyes start his managerial career?

111. Patrice Evra was born in which country?

112. Having suffered five defeats in the league by 1 December 2001, critics were quick to point out that the losses had been against teams where by the first letters spelt out his surname: Bolton Wanderers, Liverpool, Arsenal, Newcastle United, and Chelsea. Who is it?

113.   Which former United player was voted Swedish Footballer of the Year for the second time for his performances throughout the 2003/04 season?

114.   Sir Alex Ferguson famously lost his first game in charge, but who was it against?

115.   Did Michael Carrick or Bryan Robson make more appearances for United?

FIND THE ANSWERS
ON THE
NEXT PAGE!

Round Two Answers 101-115

101. Ronnie Johnsen.
102. Red.
103. Sheffield United.
104. Mario Basler.
105. 1878.
106. Ryan Shawcross.
107. Jaap Stam.
108. Anderson.
109. Ryan Giggs.
110. Preston North End.
111. Senegal.
112. Laurent Blanc.
113. Henrik Larsson.
114. Oxford United.
115. Michael Carrick.

Round Two Quiz Questions 116-130:

116. Who replaced Fabien Barthez as United's first-choice goalkeeper?

117. Two united players were nicknamed "Dolly and Daisy", who were they?

118. The winning goal in the 1996 F.A. Cup Final was scored by whom?

119. What is the name of Gary and Phil Neville's father?

120. "Butch" was the nickname of which former United player?

121. Which former United player became head coach of the Ecuador national football team?

122. How many goals did Wayne Rooney score for United in his 559 appearances?

123. Which player got into trouble after stealing a doughnut?

124. Man Utd's biggest loss came at the hands of Wolverhampton Wanderers on 26 September 1953?

125. Who made their debut for United on 13 August 2017 in a 4-0 win over West Ham United and earned himself a Man of the Match award?

126. Which former German international who netted 24 times for his country went onto play for Chicago Fire after United?

127. This former United "Super Sub" came on the pitch in the 72nd minute and scored four goals in twelve minutes against Nottingham Forest. Who was it?

128. In the 1974/75 season, which team did United draw 2-2 with

to confirm their Second Division championship and promotion back to the top flight of football?

129. Who scored United's goal against Liverpool in the 1-0 victory in the 1979 F.A. Cup Semi-Final replay?

130. Which ex-United legend had a liver transplant in 2002?

FIND THE ANSWERS
ON THE
NEXT PAGE!

Round Two Answers 116-130

116.   Tim Howard.
117.   Steve Bruce and Gary Pallister.
118.   Eric Cantona.
119.   Neville Neville.
120.   Ray Wilkins.
121.   Jordi Cruyff.
122.   253.
123.   David De Gea.
124.   8-1.
125.   Nemanja Matić.
126.   Bastian Schweinsteiger.
127.   Ole Gunnar Solskjær.
128.   Notts County.
129.   Jimmy Greenhoff.
130.   George Best.

Round Two Quiz Questions 131-150:

131. From which club was Danish goalkeeper Peter Schmeichel acquired?

132. Manchester United won the 2000/01 Premier League campaign by 10 points, but who scored the only goal of the game as Liverpool became the first team to beat United at home?

133. At which stadium did Dwight Yorke make his United debut?

134. Who was sent off after fouling Mario Balotelli in United's 6-1 defeat to Manchester City?

135. Who did Louis van Gaal place on the transfer list on 15 July 2015 for allegedly refusing to play in a reserve match?

136. The Premier League's 25,000th goal was scored by which superstar?

137. Who was the first United manager from outside of England?

138. Due to participation in the FIFA Club World Championship, what year did United withdraw from the F.A. Cup?

139. Which United player was in France's World Cup winning team in 2018?

140. The first United manager from outside of the United Kingdom was whom?

141. After a spell as an assistant at Valencia, which former United player took the position of England's head coach for the women's team?

142. The winning goal for United in the second leg of the 1999 Semi-Final contest against Juventus was scored by which

striker?

143. What year did United sign Paul Ince from West Ham United?

144. Following their 1968 European Cup win, who did United lose to the following year in the World Club Championships?

145. Which manager signed Bryan Robson?

146. Who did United beat 2-1 in the UEFA Cup Winners' Cup Final in the 1990/91 season with two goals from Mark Hughes?

147. Roy Keane admitted setting out to purposely injure which Manchester City player in 2001?

148. Who netted their 100th goal for United in the 2004 season?

149. Where did Andrei Kanchelskis move to after leaving United?

150. Brian McClair joined United from which club?

FIND THE ANSWERS
ON THE
NEXT PAGE!

Round Two Answers 131-150

131. Brøndby.
132. Danny Murphy.
133. Upton Park.
134. Johnny Evans.
135. Victor Valdés.
136. Zlatan Ibrahimovic.
137. Scott Duncan.
138. 1999/00.
139. Paul Pogba.
140. Frank O'Farrell.
141. Phil Neville.
142. Andy Cole.
143. 1989.
144. Estudiantes.
145. Ron Atkinson.
146. Mark Hughes.
147. Alf-Inge Håland.
148. Ruud van Nistelrooy.
149. Everton.
150. Celtic.

Round Two Quiz Questions 151-165:

151. United had two players in France's 1998 World Cup winning team, who were they?

152. Sir Matt Busby spent most of his playing career at which club?

153. Who scored the Premier League's first ever goal for Sheffield United in a 2-1 win against Manchester United?

154. What is Sir Alex Ferguson's middle name?

155. Where did United loan Odion Ighalo from?

156. The first ever Premier League goal for United was scored by whom?

157. In November 2009, Alex Ferguson received a four match touchline ban for accusing which referee of being unfit?

158. Which assistant coach left United to become the manager of Blackburn Rovers in 1998?

159. Who won the European Footballer of the Year in 2008?

160. Which band took United to top of the pop charts in 1994 with "Come on You Reds"?

161. Where did United finish in the 2018/19 campaign?

162. Which former United striker began their career at Feyenoord and netted 50 times for Holland?

163. Who took over from David Moyes as manager for the remaining games of the 2013/14 season?

164. Which former United right back started his career with El Nacional?

165. On the 5th October 2014, which player scored his first goal for United in a 2-1 home victory against Everton?

FIND THE ANSWERS
ON THE
NEXT PAGE!

Round Two Answers 151-165

151. Laurent Blanc and Fabien Barthez.
152. Manchester City.
153. Brian Deane.
154. Chapman.
155. Shanghai Greenland Shenhua.
156. Mark Hughes.
157. Alan Wiley.
158. Brian Kidd.
159. Cristiano Ronaldo.
160. Status Quo.
161. Sixth.
162. Robin van Persie.
163. Ryan Giggs.
164. Antonio Valencia.
165. Radamel Falcao.

Round Two Quiz Questions

166.   Who became the world's most expensive defender?

167.   What is the devil holding on the Man Utd badge?

168.   After the death of Sir Matt Busby in 1994, United played Everton and were 1-0 winners. Who scored that winning goal?

169.   Who did Sir Alex Ferguson once admit to being his worst signing?

170.   Which team ended United's European Cup pursuit at the Semi-Final stage in 1998?

171.   On 30 August 2019, which player joined AS Roma on loan?

172.   From which team did United purchase Fred?

173.   Which former United player played in three European Cup Championships, and was named in the Team of the Tournament at UEFA Euro 1996 after helping the Czechs to the final?

174.   After attacking a Belgian referee during a spell with Royal Antwerp, which player received an initial ban for life (which was later reduced)?

175.   Which former United player made three international appearances for Gibraltar?

176.   Before joining West Ham United on a free transfer at the beginning of the 2004/05 season, this player scored two goals for United after coming up through the youth system. Who is he?

177.   Which former decorated United manager spent most of his

playing career at Sparta Rotterdam?

178.   Who made his competitive debut for United in 2019 after coming on as a substitute and scoring United's final goal against Chelsea in a 4-0 win?

179.   Which former United defender assisted Cristiano Ronaldo's goal in the 2008 Champions League Final?

180.   As of 2020, who serves as United's global ambassador?

FIND THE ANSWERS
ON THE
NEXT PAGE!

Round Two Answers 166-180

166.   Harry Maguire.
167.   Fork.
168.   Ryan Giggs.
169.   Ralph Milne.
170.   Borussia Dortmund.
171.   Chris Smalling.
172.   Shakhtar Donesk.
173.   Karel Porborský.
174.   Ronnie Wallwork.
175.   Danny Higginbotham.
176.   Luke Chadwick.
177.   Louis van Gaal.
178.   Daniel James.
179.   Wes Brown.
180.   Park Ji-Sung.

Round Two Quiz Questions 181-200:

181. How many league titles have United won?

182. What year did United win their first F.A. Cup?

183. Where did Marouane Fellaini begin his footballing career?

184. Which feeder club did United start a relationship with back in 1998?

185. United signed Gabriel Heinze from where?

186. Victor Lindelöf made his United debut against which team?

187. Finish the song "Ooh Aah…"

188. Who served 18 months in jail for a counterfeit currency scandal whereby laundering money through Wrexham's trainees?

189. Which late American billionaire took over United in 2005?

190. What is the name of the Manchester United super-fan who became an internet sensation for his angry post-match rants?

191. Arsenal secured a heart-breaking victory at Old Trafford in March 1998 which led to Arsenal winning the title that year. Which Arsenal player grabbed the winning goal?

192. One former Manchester United player played in the Manchester, Merseyside, and Old Firm derbies. Who was it?

193. Several former United players, including the Neville's and David Beckham co-own a team. What club is it?

194. On the last day of the 1995/96 season, which team did United beat 3-0 to claim the title?

195. Which club have Bobby Charlton, Nobby Stiles, and Brian Kidd all managed?

196. United signed a Chinese player from Dalian Shide, who was it?

197. Who is Bulgaria's all-time leading scorer?

198. After playing a handful of games in his first spell with United, who did Mark Bosnich leave Old Trafford for?

199. Which player was sent off for United against York City in 1995 and never played for United again?

200. Schmeichel, Irwin, May, Pallister, Keane, Beckham, Butt, Giggs, Cole, Cantona and which other player started the 1996 F.A. Cup Final?

FIND THE ANSWERS
ON THE
NEXT PAGE!

Round Two Answers 181-200

181.   20.
182.   1909.
183.   Standard Liège.
184.   Royal Antwerp.
185.   Paris Saint Germain.
186.   Real Madrid.
187.   Paul McGrath.
188.   Mickey Thomas.
189.   Malcolm Glazer.
190.   Andy Tate.
191.   Marc Overmars.
192.   Andrei Kanchelskis.
193.   Salford City Football Club.
194.   Middlesbrough.
195.   Preson North End.
196.   Dong Fangzhuo.
197.   Dimitar Berbatov.
198.   Sydney Croatia (Sydney United 58)
199.   Pat McGibbon.
200.   Phil Neville.

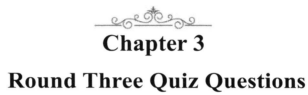

Chapter 3
Round Three Quiz Questions

Round Three Quiz Questions 201-215:

201. Where did United sign Mike Phelan from?

202. On September 1956, United pummeled Anderlecht 10-0. Which player netted 4 times?

203. L.A. Galaxy loaned David Beckham to which club?

204. After a successful career with Vitesse Arnhem, which Dutch player moved to United well into his 30's?

205. Which team did Peter Schmeichel score his only goal for United against?

206. During the 1998/99 Champions League Final against Bayern Munich, which two players did goal scorers Teddy Sheringham and Ole Gunnar Solskjær come on to replace?

207. Which television pundit declared "You can't win anything with kids" about United and Sir Alex Ferguson at the start of the 1995/96 Premier League Winning campaign?

208. Shinji Kagawa scored a hat-trick against which team?

209. Where did United sign Gordon McQueen from?

210. On 6th February 2020, which former United and Republic of Ireland player signed a 6 month contract with Salford City?

211. What age was Mason Greenwood when he first joined United as a kid?

212. Eric Bailly began his playing career at which club?

213. Bryan Robson and which other player arrived from West Bromwich Albion in the autumn of 1981?

214. Juan Mata scored his first goal for United in a 4-1 win against which club?

215. How many trophies did Jose Mourinho win at United?

FIND THE ANSWERS
ON THE
NEXT PAGE!

Round Three Answers 201-215

201.   Norwich City.
202.   Dennis Viollet.
203.   AC Milan.
204.   Raimond van der Gouw.
205.   Rotor Volgograd.
206.   Jesper Blomqvist and Andy Cole.
207.   Alan Hansen.
208.   Norwich City.
209.   Leeds United.
210.   Darren Gibson.
211.   Six.
212.   Espanyol.
213.   Remi Moses.
214.   Aston Villa.
215.   Three.

Round Three Quiz Questions 216-230:

216. Which former United player began his career at Anderlecht, netting 33 times for them before moving to England?

217. During the unforgettable clash between Roy Keane and Patrick Vieira in the tunnel at Highbury, who was playing in goal for United?

218. Who admitted changing the television channel to X-Factor and hiding the remote control in a hotel to prevent Roy Keane from watching Rugby League?

219. This former United player made one appearance in the Premier League before moving on to Preston North End, he also netted 36 times for Northern Ireland. Who is he?

220. Who was manager of England when Paul Parker won his first cap?

221. Gary Neville was born in which City?

222. In September 2017, which former United player announced his intention to become a professional boxer?

223. Tahith Chong began his youth career at which Dutch club?

224. Who signed for United on 6th June 2018 for a fee of £19 million?

225. In February 2000, which player was under investigation by the Italian police for a possible false passport in order to avoid the non-EU quota?

226. Who was United manager before Ron Atkinson?

227. David Moyes started his playing career at which club?

228. Which former United and West Ham United goalkeeper died at the age of 43?

229. Who became the first black player to start a game for the England senior side?

230. Before the Munich Air Disaster, which player was captain of United?

FIND THE ANSWERS
ON THE
NEXT PAGE!

Round Three Answers 216-230

216.   Romelu Lukaku.
217.   Roy Carroll.
218.   Wayne Rooney.
219.   David Healy.
220.   Bobby Robson.
221.   Bury.
222.   Rio Ferdinand.
223.   Feyenoord.
224.   Diogo Dalot.
225.   Juan Sebastián Verón.
226.   Dave Sexton.
227.   Celtic.
228.   Les Sealey.
229.   Viv Anderson.
230.   Roger Byrne.

Round Three Quiz Questions 231-250:

231. Ryan Giggs holds the award for United appearances, but what year did he retire?

232. Which player had the nickname "The Guv'nor"?

233. When "the Busby Babes" won back to back titles in 1956 and 1957, what was the average age of the squad?

234. What year was the devil incorporated into the club crest?

235. In which year was the crest including the devil placed onto a United shirt?

236. To the nearest thousand, what is Old Trafford's capacity?

237. According to the global market research agency Kantar, what is the figure of United's worldwide fan and follower base?

238. What year did United become a listed company where they sold shares to local supporters for £1 per share?

239. Who is United's oldest player as of the 2019/20 season?

240. Sir Alex Ferguson hired which assistant manager when he joined United?

241. Which team did United beat in 1991 to lift their UEFA Super Cup victory?

242. What were Newton Heath's kit colours when they played their first ever recorded match in 1880?

243. During United's treble winning campaign in the 1998/99 season, which three trophies did they win?

244. What ground did United play at during the first 15 years of

their history?

245. In which year did United lift their first ever Charity Shield?

246. During the 1981/82 season, United had two players who played in every single game, who were they?

247. Who scored for United in their 1-0 win in the 1999 Intercontinental cup victory over Palmeiras.

248. United's best ever start to a league campaign saw them win 10 games on the bounce. Who was in charge?

249. Who was the first German that United fielded in the first team?

250. Denis Law was the first player that United signed from Torino, and there has only been one further signing to date. Who was it?

FIND THE ANSWERS
ON THE
NEXT PAGE!

231. 2014.
232. Paul Ince.
233. 22.
234. 1970.
235. 1971.
236. 76,000.
237. 1.1 billion.
238. 1892.
239. Lee Grant.
240. Archie Knox.
241. Red Star Belgrade.
242. Green and gold.
243. Premier League, F.A. Cup, Champions League.
244. North Road.
245. 1909.
246. Arthur Albiston and Ray Wilkins.
247. Roy Keane.
248. Ron Atkinson.
249. Bastian Schweinsteiger.
250. Matteo Darmian.

Round Three Quiz Questions 251-265:

251. In November 2001, Fabien Barthez played mind games by standing aside from the goal with his hands held behind his back during a penalty causing the opposing player to miss. Who was the Leicester City player who missed the spot kick?

252. How many consecutive clean sheets did Sergio Romero keep in his first Premier League appearances?

253. Where did United sign Anders Lindegaard from?

254. In United's treble winning season in 1999, which player won PFA an FWA player of the season awards?

255. Which United player scored in every Premier League season up until his retirement?

256. In 2013/14 season, which United player averaged 4.3 shots per game in the Premier League according to whoscored.com?

257. How many times did United win the F.A. Cup in the 1990's?

258. Who wore number 18 for United in the 2019/20 season?

259. Where did United finish in Louis van Gaal's first season?

260. Which company is the official carrier of United as of 2020?

261. Who had a stint at Mumbai City F.C. in 2016?

262. Darren Ferguson moved onto which club after playing for United?

263. Owen Hargreaves went on to play for England at International level but who did he represent at U19 level?

264.   Which former United player provided the cross which set up
        Marco van Basten's unbelievable volley in the European
        Championships in 1988 against the Soviet Union?

265.   Three former United players won the World Cup in 2010 and
        European Championships in 2012 with Spain. Who are they?

FIND THE ANSWERS
ON THE
NEXT PAGE!

Round Three Answers 251-265

251. Muzzy Izzet.
252. Three.
253. Aalesund.
254. David Ginola.
255. Ryan Giggs.
256. Robin van Persie.
257. 4.
258. Bruno Fernandes.
259. 4th.
260. Aeroflot.
261. Diego Forlán.
262. Wolverhampton Wanderers.
263. Wales U19's.
264. Arnold Mühren.
265. Gerard Piqué, Juan Mata, Victor Valdés.

Round Three Quiz Questions 266-280:

266. Carlos Tevez played for which Brazilian team in the 2005/06 season?

267. When Marcus Rojo joined United in August 2014 from Sporting, who moved the opposite way on a season long loan?

268. The number 8 shirt in the 2004/05 season was worn by which player?

269. Which Hungarian side knocked United out of the UEFA Cup on penalties in the 1984/85 season?

270. From which team did United sign Alex Stepney?

271. Which player had a 17-year spell with United and earned the nickname "The Gunner" because of his prolific goalscoring?

272. Sir Matt Busby's final signing in 1969 was which Northern Irishman?

273. Who did Andy Cole score his one and only goal for England against?

274. "Give it to Joe" was a commonly heard terrace chant during which players' 14 years at Old Trafford?

275. When Marcus Rashford first got called up to the England squad, who was manager?

276. Which two former United players were in Denmark's European Championship winning team of 1992?

277. Park Ji-Sung joined United from which club?

278. How old was Ashley Januzaj when he left Anderlecht for

United?

279. Twin brothers Fábio and Rafael began their youth careers at which Brazilian club?

280. Which former United player is Mexico's all-time leading scorer?

FIND THE ANSWERS
ON THE
NEXT PAGE!

Round Three Answers 266-280

266. Corinthians.
267. Nani.
268. Wayne Rooney.
269. Videoton.
270. Chelsea.
271. Jack Rowley.
272. Sammy McIlroy.
273. Albania.
274. Joe Spence.
275. Roy Hodgson.
276. Peter Schmeichel and John Sivebæk.
277. PSV Eindhoven.
278. 16.
279. Fluminense.
280. Javier Hernández.

Round Three Quiz Questions 281-300:

281. Who was the Premier League's top scorer in 2011?

282. Patrice Evra forced which player to lose his place?

283. Which winger joined United from Ajax in 1984 for £350,000?

284. Who won the Premier League title in each of his first full three seasons at Old Trafford before joining Lazio in a surprise move?

285. Which Englishman is the highest scorer in the Champions League with 30 goals?

286. Who is the second highest Champions League goal scorer from England with 24 goals?

287. This United goalkeeper saved three penalties in the 6-0 defeat to Ipswich Town at Portman Road in 1980, who is he?

288. Which player scored United's 1000th goal in the Premier League in 2015/16?

289. Who bagged the most hat-tricks for United with 18 total?

290. Where did Tim Howard begin his playing career?

291. The 1998 movie "Elizabeth" saw an appearance from which former United player?

292. Who scored United's first goal in the 1990 F.A. Cup Final?

293. Ole Gunnar Solskjær scored his first league goal at Old Trafford against whom?

294. How many games did United lose in their Premier League

winning season in 1999?

295. Arthur Albiston replaced which player to make his F.A. Cup debut in the 1977 victory against Liverpool?

296. Which two players were on the scoresheet when United defeated Liverpool 2-1 in the 1985 F.A. Cup Semi-Final replay?

297. Roy Keane joined United from which club?

298. In 2011, Sir Alex Ferguson ended his 7 year boycott against which organisation?

299. Which team did Cristiano Ronaldo score his only hat-trick against?

300. The infamous kung fu kick at a fan by Eric Cantona occurred at which stadium?

FIND THE ANSWERS
ON THE
NEXT PAGE!

281. Dimitar Berbatov.
282. Gabriel Heinze.
283. Jesper Olsen.
284. Jaap Stam.
285. Wayne Rooney.
286. Paul Scholes.
287. Gary Bailey.
288. Anthony Martial.
289. Denis Law.
290. North Jersey Imperials.
291. Eric Cantona.
292. Bryan Robson.
293. Blackburn Rovers.
294. 3.
295. Stewart Houston.
296. Bryan Robson and Mark Hughes.
297. Nottingham Forest.
298. The BBC.
299. Newcastle United.
300. Selhurst Park.

One Last Thing

If you have enjoyed this book, please don't forget to write a **review** of this publication. It is really useful feedback as well as providing untold encouragement to the author.